# Australia
## in colour

*Endpapers: Tooloom Falls, near Urbenville,*
*New South Wales*
*Next page: River red gums, Flinders Ranges,*
*South Australia*

# ROBIN SMITH'S
# Australia
## in colour

**Currey, O'Neil**

# A vast country

## The natural landscapes are still unspoiled

Man has barely left his mark on Australia.

No other continent except Antarctica has such vast tracts of virgin territory, such expanses of uninhabited land where nature may be seen untouched by the inroads of civilization.

Before the first European settlers came in 1788, Australia's comparatively small number of Aborigines lived in harmony with their environment; they tilled no crops, grazed no animals, built none but the most temporary structures. They were nomadic people who left for the casual observer no evidence of their passing.

In the 200 years since their arrival Australia's European settlers have certainly made a larger visual impact, but it has been both concentrated and marginal. Four in five white Australians live in the continent's coastal cities. Most of the others are concentrated into a few fertile areas: the coastal strips and the rich plains immediately behind the ranges of the east, south-east and south-west coasts.

Australia is a dry continent, half of it with a median rainfall of less than 300 millimetres a year, four-fifths of it with less than 600 millimetres a year. It is a hot continent, too, with 39 per cent of its land surface in the tropics and most of the remainder in the sub-tropics. Temperatures often reach 50°C or more in the inland.

Taken overall, Australia is flat, hot and dry. But it is large enough and diverse enough to have parts that are far from flat, parts that are far from hot, parts that are far from dry.

Australia's highest, best known and most imposing mountains are in the Great Dividing Range that runs like a gigantic backbone not far inland from the east coast.

*Left: Fitzroy Falls near Moss Vale, New South Wales*

It includes the jungle-clad mountains of Queensland, the Blue Mountains of New South Wales, and the vast Australian Alps of the south-east. Other impressive and picturesque mountains are to be found in Tasmania, in the Flinders Ranges of South Australia, in the Musgrave and MacDonnell Ranges of the Red Centre, in the Darling Range of Western Australia.

The vast expanses of snow-covered mountains in the south-east deny the suggestion that Australia is always and everywhere hot. So too do the south-east and south-west corners of the continent, and the island state of Tasmania, which are relatively temperate.

Australia has some notable exceptions to its dryness too. Compared with the continental low average rainfall, which reaches its minimum of about 100 millimetres east of Lake Eyre, the tropical east coast of Queensland (at Tully) has 4400 millimetres, the west coast of Tasmania (at Lake Margaret) 3600 millimetres.

Australia is a land of few large rivers and water is a prized commodity. Perhaps this is why Australians see such beauty in their waterways, and will listen endlessly to schemes to irrigate the vast inland without bothering to enquire too closely into the economics.

Most of the rivers rise in the Great Dividing Range of the east. Some flow along short rapid courses towards the Pacific Coast. Others meander generally south-west to become part of the giant Murray-Darling system. Some flow north-west into the Gulf of Carpentaria. Still others filter into nothingness in the sands of the Red Centre. There are great rivers too in the north, particularly in the Northern Territory, born of torrential tropical rains.

*Autumn morning, Lake Wendouree,*
*Ballarat, Victoria*
*Next pages: Mount Sonder, MacDonnell*
*Ranges, Northern Territory*

6

*Mount Cooroy landscape,
Queensland*

# Scenic coastline

Beaches and bays mark the Pacific's shores

Australia's east provides a nice tidy map, provided you don't look too closely at the details. The coast and the mountains usually run north-south, the rivers usually east or west.

The coast veers gently towards the right of the map until it reaches its most easterly point at Cape Byron.

Stand almost anywhere along this coast and you look out across the rolling surf of the Pacific Ocean. It has pounded much of the eastern fringe of Australia into sand, giving it one of the world's longest and most appealing lines of beaches.

Nature put some of them within easy distance of the spot where the metropolis of Sydney developed. Suburbs such as Manly, Dee Why, Avalon, Palm Beach, Coogee, Maroubra and Bondi grew up along them. Others, handier to the future city of Brisbane, evolved into the Gold Coast and the Sunshine Coast. Between these focal points the beaches go on almost uninterrupted for thousands of kilometres.

This coast of lengthy beaches and secluded bays is not punctuated by many great harbours. But there is one to rival the world's finest. When Captain James Cook sailed past it in 1770 he noted 'a bay wherein there appeared to be a safe anchorage' and called it Port Jackson. Now better known as Sydney Harbour, it is one of the busiest ports in the world, and navigable by the largest vessels afloat.

Paralleling the coast, the narrow coastal plain also lies north and south and varies in width from about 30 kilometres to about 80 kilometres. Nature clothed much of this plain with forests of eucalypts, with occasional patches of such precious timbers as cedar.

*Left: Jutting headlands of Disaster Bay, New South Wales*

In the two centuries since European settlers first arrived here they have cleared areas of this forest and cultivated pastures, citrus orchards, vineyards and banana plantations in the southern (New South Wales) part, and pineapples, bananas and sugar cane in the northern (Queensland) part.

Directly inland from the coastal plain, again with a general north-south alignment, runs the Great Dividing Range; in reality a series of ranges and more accurately described as the eastern highlands.

The mountains of the Great Divide are not particularly high by world standards for Australia is an ancient continent and her peaks are well-worn.

The greatness of the range lies in its role as a giant watershed, determining the flow direction of major rivers, supplying the entire eastern side of the continent.

The Blue Mountains are among the maverick spurs that here and there break the north-south pattern and shoot off at an angle from the main range, in their case to the east. The McPherson Range that forms some of the border between New South Wales and Queensland is another rugged spur that pushes east. In northern New South Wales the Liverpool Range runs westwards to culminate in the striking pinnacles and spires of the Warrumbungle Range.

In other places the Great Dividing Range flattens out and broadens into such tablelands as the Darling Downs of southern Queensland and the New England Tableland of northern New South Wales.

Beyond the fertile tablelands and western slopes of the ranges lie the great western plains where Australia's national emblems, the kangaroo and the emu, roam and where the wheatfields of the Golden West soon give way to the Red Centre.

*Spectacular Ebor Falls, New England,*
*New South Wales*

*Hanging Rock, Shoalhaven River,*
*Nowra, New South Wales*

On the remote and ruggedly beautiful
seaward edge of the New England
tablelands the Guy Fawkes River ends with
a splash at the spectacular Ebor Falls, near
the town of Ebor. There are many fast,
clear streams with cascades and waterfalls
in this New England region, the largest
area of highland in Australia, covering
some 14 500 square kilometres.

The Hanging Rock juts out over the
Shoalhaven River at Nowra, a large coastal
town south of Sydney. The Shoalhaven is
wide and ideal for fishing and boating at its
mouth, but in the densely-forested country
of the Moreton National Park it becomes a
swift-flowing race. Ben's Walk runs from
Hanging Rock to a suspension bridge over
Nowra Creek, said to be the first bridge of
its kind constructed in Australia.

The Bellinger River near Fernmount,
New South Wales

*Quiet pool on the Tenterfield River,
New South Wales*

*Mount Lindesay's ancient volcanic
cone, southern Queensland*

The Tenterfield River, near the town of
Tenterfield, is a feature of the scenically
lovely New England countryside in a region
where introduced willows shade the many
small streams. Tenterfield celebrates the
Festival of the Willows in late summer. In
1889 the Australian statesman Sir Henry
Parkes made a speech at the Tenterfield
School of Arts which is regarded as having
launched the movement for Federation.

Mount Lindesay, near the New South
Wales-Queensland border, rises to a height
of 1239 metres. Like the Glasshouse
Mountains further north, it is part of an old
volcanic cone, the core of which has been
gradually exposed and eroded. The
mountain forms part of the MacPherson
Range, whose dark bulk is covered by thick,
sub-tropical forests. The range contains
many vivid flowering trees and orchids.

*The Three Sisters, Blue Mountains, New South Wales*

*Purlingbrook Falls, Springbrook, southern Queensland*

The Blue Mountains are, from a distance, an intense cobalt blue. Spectacular sandstone precipices ring the densely wooded valleys and the rugged terrain is broken by deep gorges. The Three Sisters at Katoomba are the best-known landmark of the mountains. These remarkable towers of weathered sandstone rise more than 457 metres above their talus slopes in the Jamieson Valley, west of Sydney.

Although comparatively small, the Springbrook National Park, 120 kilometres from Brisbane, contains a wealth of rocky gorges, water courses, mountain slopes and a rich bird life. Purlingbrook Falls, with their deep viridian pool and jungle-covered amphitheatre where many arboreal orchids flower, provide one of the most delightful spots in the park.

*Sydney Harbour, Port Jackson,
New South Wales*

*Dawes Point Park and harbour bridge,
Sydney, New South Wales*

Sydney, the capital of New South Wales and Australia's largest city, is built around one of the world's finest harbours. The 290 kilometres of rocky foreshore twist into a ragged coastline forming numerous small beaches, coves, bays and headlands. Flanking the harbour entrance, the rollers of the Pacific ocean crash on to rocky cliffs and stretches of golden sand.

Sydney's great landmark, the stark meccano-like structure of the Harbour Bridge, still towers above the high-rise buildings of the city. The second-largest single span structure in the world, it measures 503 metres from pylon to pylon, and the actual roadway is suspended 135 metres above the water from the bold arch. Built between 1923 and 1932, the bridge handles a huge daily traffic flow.

23

*Morning and misty landscape,
Coff's Harbour*

*Belougery Spire, Warrumbungle Mountains, New South Wales*

*Rock spires, Warrumbungles National Park, New South Wales*

A magnificent place of refuge for wildlife in the surrounding farmland of the western slopes, the Warrumbungles National Park is dramatised by the spires of old mountains, which give rise to gorge-cut country and lush vegetation. One formation is Belougery Spire, which towers amid a group of peaks and can be reached by walking trail. The peaks go through colour changes as the sun's rays sweep them.

The Warrumbungles National Park, west of Coonabarabran in central-west New South Wales, contains some of Australia's most spectacular scenery. The mountains are the remains of volcanic eruptions, but the cones and craters are gone, worn away by the streams which now flow through gorges and valleys of the park. The major features of the jagged knot of spires, domes and mesas can be seen from the Grand High Tops.

*The Needles formation, Gibraltar Range, New South Wales*

*The Manning River and Mount George, New South Wales*

'The Needles' is a landmark of the Gibraltar Range, a granite plateau which forms the eastern escarpment of the New England Plateau. The range contains a great area of magnificent scenery, but it is a rugged, gorge-cut region, much of which is inaccessible to all but experienced bush walkers. Its heathlands are rich in wildflowers.

The Manning River has its origins in the rugged Mount Royal Range and flows east to empty into the Pacific Ocean at Harrington Inlet. On its 200 kilometre journey to the sea, the Manning winds through rich farmlands supporting wheat, maize, vegetables and dairying. In places its broad banks are heavily timbered while in others virgin bush gives way to broad, sandy river flats.

*Sheep on the track, near Cooma,
New South Wales*

*Lake Glenbawn, near Scone, Hunter Valley, New South Wales*

*Slopes of rugged Mount Lindesay, southern Queensland*

Sprawled amid the slopes of the Hunter River Valley, the Glenbawn Dam serves to alleviate the flooding to which the area was prone. The dam harnesses the waters of the Hunter and its tributaries for irrigation for farmlands and for the vineyards which produce some of Australia's finest wines. A national park has been proclaimed in an area of bushland adjacent to the lake formed by the dam.

Mount Lindesay's dark bulk broods over the New South Wales-Queensland border. It is the highest peak in the MacPherson Range, part of which is in the Lamington National Park. The mountain was partly climbed in 1827 by Captain Patrick Logan who mistakenly believed it to be Mount Warning which Cook had sighted and named when the *Endeavour* narrowly escaped being wrecked off Point Danger.

*Blooms of Golden Wattle;
national floral emblem*

*The Gold of Autumn, Cotter Reserve,
Australian Capital Territory*

Australia's national floral emblem is the *Acacia,* commonly known as wattle. There are more than 600 different species of this plant, ranging in size from straggly shrubs to small trees, and well distributed from the tropical north to the cooler south. Wherever the wattle grows, its dense clusters of bright yellow blossom give a welcome splash of colour to the surrounding greens and browns of the bush.

Conceived and developed as the nation's capital, Canberra has had the advantage of total and enlightened planning which has made it both the most formal and most handsome of Australian cities. Visitors sometimes find it cold and impersonal but there is beauty and stimulation in the impressive public buildings, an aesthetic nicety of order and spaciousness in its suburbs and a grandeur in its gardens.

*'Skyway' at Katoomba, Blue
Mountains, New South Wales*

*Bridge near Crystal Falls,
Paluma, Queensland*

A popular way to see the beautiful scenery of the Blue Mountains is by the skyway at Katoomba, which operates from a spot near the Katoomba Falls and runs on a cable strung between cliff faces 300 metres above the valley. Some of the major features in the mountains are Mount Solitary, the Ruined Castle, King's Tableland, Orphan Rock, the Bridal Veil and Leura Cascades.

At Moongobulla the road from Townsville to the Mount Spec National Park turns westward and runs through the Paluma Ranges, offering spectacular views of coastal farms and off-shore islands. In the Crystal Gorge the road crosses this charming bridge that spans the sparkling waters of the Crystal Creek. The mottled shades of its undressed stone blend pleasingly with the surrounding rain-forest.

*Fishing boats at the wharf, Eden, New South Wales*

*The Bellinger River near Thora,*
*New South Wales*

*The Orara River at Coramba,*
*New South Wales*

It would be hard to find landscapes of more tranquil beauty than those along parts of the Bellinger Valley. After their first headlong flight from the forested slopes of the Dorrigo Plateau, the waters of the Bellinger River move so placidly that they mirror the parklike banks flanking the river's meandering course. Contentment and plenty flow through the landscape like the lazy river itself.

The Orara River flows through the beautiful hinterland behind Coff's Harbour, where tree-lined rivers wind through soft pastures to the sea, framed against the ranges tinged a deep and luminous blue. The small inland towns like Coramba nestle in a gentle landscape, but further inland the country becomes wilder, shadowed by hoop pine, black butt and ironbark.

*Brisbane and sweep of the Brisbane River, Queensland*

*The Observatory, Brisbane's oldest building, Queensland*

The discovery and development of natural resources has given Queensland a rapid rate of economic growth. To its established rural produce of beef, grain, wool, sugar, fruit, dairy produce, peanuts, tobacco and timber has been added the new riches from the ground. Its capital, Brisbane, reflects this growth in new buildings and the lively, confident air that permeates its once somnolent streets.

This building has had a varied existence. It was built in 1829 as a windmill but a fault prevented the sails from working and it was used as a treadmill by convicts. It was sold in 1849 but reclaimed and used as a government signal station. It became an observatory in 1882 and was used to signal Standard Time after 1894. Today it houses a museum of relics.

Gordonville and Dorrigo
Mountains, New South Wales

*Beach and rock formations at Narooma, New South Wales*

*Rock fishing at Bermagui, New South Wales*

The section of the beautiful southern coast near Narooma has made the town known for its excellent big-game fishing grounds. There are many lakes and inlets around the town, and a coastline with beautiful rock pools and dramatic rock formations. The rich surrounding district is noted for dairying, maize production and timber. 'Narooma' derives from an Aboriginal word meaning 'clear blue water'.

Like nearby Narooma, the little town of Bermagui is well known as a big-game fishing resort. The waters of the continental shelf at this point abound with fish, and visitors can enjoy the thrill of reeling in snapper, tuna or Australian salmon. The rocky, ocean coastline of Bermagui and the neighbouring coastal town of Eden can be treacherous for swimmers but provides splendid opportunities for the fisherman.

*Female Grey Kangaroo and joey*

*The Koala, popular native marsupial*

There are about 40 species of kangaroo, the largest being the Great Grey Kangaroo or Forester, and the Red, or Plains Kangaroo. Grey Kangaroos have been known to measure more than 2.5 metres from the nose to the tip of the tail. The young are born at a very early stage of development, and the 'joeys' are suckled and protected in a pouch on the female's abdomen until they are old enough to fend for themselves.

This endearing tree-dwelling marsupial is found in forest country in some eastern and south-eastern regions of Australia. It will eat only the leaves and shoots of about a dozen varieties of eucalypt, and for many years attempts to keep it in captivity were unsuccessful. Now, the koala is a favourite at nature reserves and sanctuaries. Its soft, grey fur, leathery nose and beady eyes give it the appearance of a small bear.

*Ebor Falls, Ebor, New England,*
*New South Wales*

*Arm of the Maroochy River near*
*Yandina, Queensland*

The New England tableland abounds in
swift-flowing rivers, clear streams and
spectacular waterfalls. The dramatically
beautiful Ebor Falls are found
80 kilometres north of Armidale, centre of
this rich pastoral and agricultural district.
Produce of the region includes wool,
fat lambs, beef cattle, maize, barley, corn,
oats, vegetables and fruit and dairy
products.

The Maroochy River flows south through
Yandina, then south-east into the Pacific
Ocean near Maroochydore. Although during
the middle of last century it was used for
transporting valuable timber from the forest
of the hinterland, it now flows peacefully
through sugar canefields and tropical fruit
plantations. The Wappa Dam has been
built on the Maroochy River to supply the
nearby towns.

**The Opera House, Bennelong Point,
Sydney, New South Wales**

The sail-like contours of the harbourside
Opera House reflect the spirit of Sydney:
a love of the sea, open air and sailing, the
soaring optimism of a still young society
and an aspiration towards a vigorous
culture. Designed by the Dane Joern
Utzon, the Opera House is considered one
of the most notable architectural
achievements of the twentieth century. It is
a spectacular sight, framed against the blue
waters and sky of a bright Sydney day.

*Sunrise at quiet Pittwater on Broken Bay, New South Wales*

*Yachts on Sydney Harbour, New South Wales*

Pittwater is a large bay stretching south-east of the Hawkesbury mouth, and reputedly one of the finest stretches of boating water in the world; a scene for idyllic weekends and holidays for Sydney's great army of boat-owners. Ocean-going yachts and cruisers sail up from Sydney Harbour to swell the ranks of the local boats but there is plenty of water for all — a maze of bays and inlets.

The Harbour (officially named Port Jackson) is the focal point of Sydney. It is the busiest port in the South Pacific and has a fleet of ferries, supplemented by high-speed hydrofoils, which carries commuters between the city and the North Shore suburbs. Hundreds of private yachts shelter in its coves, and on fine days the deep blue waters are dotted with sails.

*Banana Bowl area, Coff's Harbour,*
*New South Wales*

*Pineapple crop and Mount Tibrogargan,*
*southern Queensland*

Once famous for its red cedar exports, the area around Coff's Harbour is now mainly used for the growing of bananas and other tropical fruits and vegetables. As the dense red cedar forests were cleared, the country was ploughed and patch-worked with fields and orchards. However, valuable veneering timbers are still milled in the nearby mountains, and Coff's Harbour remains a major timber shipping port.

Mount Tibrogargan, reaching a height of 282 metres, is one of the main peaks of the spectacular Glasshouse Mountains just north of Brisbane. Being of volcanic origin, the surrounding countryside is very rich and grows fine crops of pineapples as well as producing timber and tobacco.

*Tweed River landscape and Mount Warning, New South Wales*

*Bobbin Head anchorage, Ku-ring-gai Chase, Sydney, New South Wales*

The 1158-metre peak of Mount Warning dominates the Tweed River landscape in north-eastern New South Wales. Some of the most gentle and classically pastoral scenery in Australia is to be found here on the border of New South Wales and Queensland. The land produces sugar and tropical fruit, grown on farms cut out of the forest. Valuable timber is still to be found in the mist-filled valleys of the ranges.

Bobbin Head is a favourite anchorage for boating enthusiasts on the Hawkesbury River and its tributaries. It is situated deep in the narrow, flooded valley called Cowan's Creek which runs deep into the heart of the Ku-ring-gai Chase National Park, a magnificent bush area only 25 kilometres from the centre of Sydney. The thickly-forested plateau falls steeply in huge sandstone cliffs to the water below.

Mount Warning landscape, northern
New South Wales

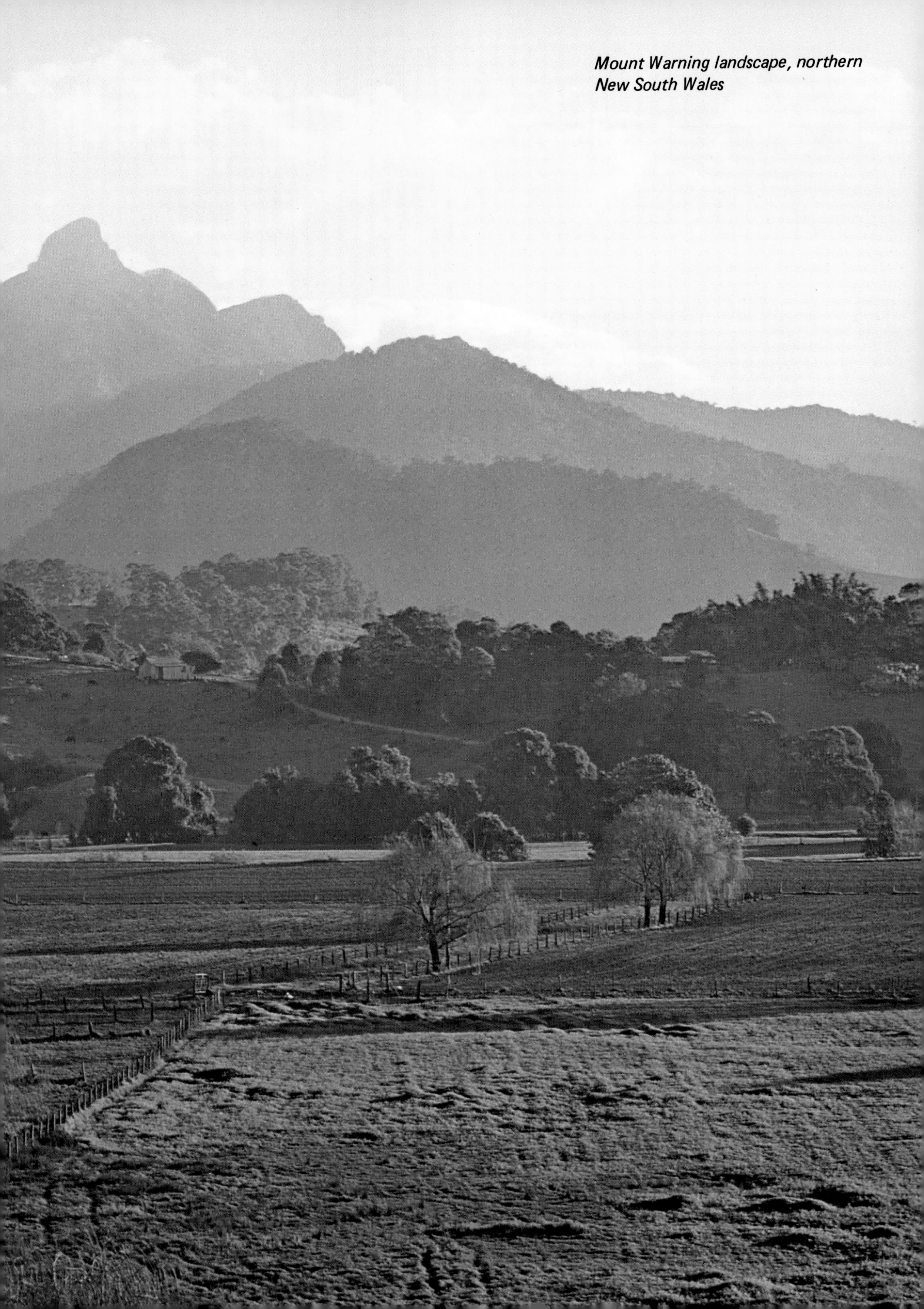

*Limpinwood landscape, northern New South Wales*

*Nerang River landscape, southern Queensland*

The hinterland behind the northern border region is dramatic country, with rainforested mountain regions jutting from rich and rolling country. The timbered landscape at Limpinwood lies between the bulk of Mount Warning and the renowned Lamington National Park. Nearby is the Limpinwood Nature Reserve.

The sparkling Nerang River rises in the MacPherson Range near Springbrook and flows down through the Numinbah Valley, past Nerang to Surfers Paradise and then into the Pacific Ocean at Southport.

*Crop of Nambour pineapples,
southern Queensland*

*Lorikeet, Currumbin Sanctuary,
southern Queensland*

In the valley surrounding Nambour, 120 kilometres north of Brisbane, rich volcanic soil yields abundant crops of pineapples and sugar cane. The area has become famous for its agricultural plantings which include banana, strawberry and ginger crops. The district is extremely popular with tourists who are able to enjoy the pleasures of both seaside and mountain resorts.

The swift-flying, brightly-coloured Rainbow Lorikeet is a common sight throughout eastern Australia. At the famous Currumbin Bird Sanctuary on the Gold Coast huge flocks of these attractive, noisy parrots swoop down, twice daily, to amuse hundreds of tourists with their antics whilst eating bread and honey from dishes and the visitors' hands, shoulders and heads.

64

Yarrunga Valley, Shoalhaven
headwaters, New South Wales

*Cape Byron, New South Wales;*
*Australia's easternmost point*

*Stanwell Park coastline from*
*Bald Hill, New South Wales*

Cape Byron, the easternmost point of the
Australian continent, is the best-known
landmark of the north-coast town of Byron
Bay. Watego's Beach, underneath the cape,
is considered one of Australia's finest
surfing beaches because of its northerly
aspect, and the town is a mecca for surfers.
Captain Cook named Cape Byron and
Byron Bay after naval explorer John Byron,
the grandfather of the poet Lord Byron.

Bald Hill, 50 kilometres south of Sydney, is
one of the best-known of the roadside
lookouts along the dramatic Illawarra
coast. Perched on towering headlands,
these offer views of golden beaches and
headlands stretching away to the horizon.

# Westerly views
## Wildflowers carpet a sun-drenched landscape

Thousands of immigrants to Australia have landed at Fremantle, intending to use it as a starting point from which to look the country over. But they have settled down to live in or near Perth because the west delivered everything they had expected of Australia: sun and sand and sea and sky.

They seem to agree with Captain James Stirling, the Royal Navy captain who explored the Swan River in 1827, that the area 'appears to hold out every attraction that a country in a state of nature can possess'. The Swan is no longer in quite the state of nature that it was in Stirling's day, but Perth is still a small enough city to be dominated by its site rather than vice versa.

The nearby countryside is green and pleasant, thanks mainly to the Darling Range, which runs parallel to the coast for about 80 kilometres north and 250 kilometres south of Perth, and encourages the winds that have swept across the Indian Ocean to drop some of their moisture on the coastal plain.

The state of Western Australia occupies about a third of the continent, but only the coastal strip in the south-west has ever succumbed to substantial European settlement. This area has a more reliable winter rainfall, mainly from May to October, and escapes the fierce summer heat that sears the north and the inland.

The rainfall is most prolonged and most adequate in the extreme south-west and much of the area is under dense forests of karri (*Eucalyptus diversicolor*), one of the world's tallest trees. In areas where the rainy season is shorter, between the Swan Valley and the karri areas, the dominant tree is jarrah (*Eucalyptus marginata*), Western Australia's most popular timber.

*Left: Karri forest near Beedelup Falls, Western Australia*

The south-west of Western Australia is not a region of great mountains. The Darling Range rarely rises above 300 metres and its highest point is Mount Cooke, at 582 metres. In places the range, the western edge of the Great Western Plateau, rises sharply from the coastal plain and rivers have cut ravines through it, providing opportunities to dam such rivers as the Canning for Perth's water supply. Water from the Mundaring Weir, on the Helena River, is pumped over 500 kilometres to Kalgoorlie and Kambalda.

It is in the south-west that most of Western Australia's famous wildflowers flourish. Visitors come to see the vivid blue leschenaultia, the delicately-fashioned kangaroo paw, and the colourful displays of banksias and heath, and to sniff the delightful aroma of brown boronia.

Visitors with limited time to sample the wildflowers of the west need go no further than King's Park, the 403 hectare bushland reserve only a few minutes walk from the heart of Perth. But those who take the time to explore further in the flowering season (September, October, November) can feast their eyes on many of the state's 6500 species of flowering plants.

The south-west has shared in Western Australia's mineral riches. The Collie coalfields have long provided all the state's needs, but the new mineral industry of the south-west is based on the extensive bauxite deposits of the Darling Range, conveniently close to the city and port facilities of Perth, Fremantle and Kwinana.

Kalgoorlie, Western Australia's famous goldfields city, is in the arid area beyond the fringes of the fertile south-west. The brown ironstone hills just south of the city are known as the Golden Mile, one of the richest storehouses of gold in the world, and still a major basis of Kalgoorlie's economy.

Gold rush hotels, Coolgardie,
Western Australia

Western Australia's capital city —
Perth, from King's Park

Town Hall and Council Chambers,
York, Western Australia

Perth shares some characteristics with
Adelaide — a site between mountains and
sea, a warm, dry climate and space in which
to expand. The West Australian capital,
however, is built on more undulating
ground on the banks of the Swan River
where it broadens into the tidal Perth Water.
One of Perth's greatest assets is the
405-hectare King's Park on high land
overlooking the centre of the city.

The Avon Valley was one of the first settled
regions of Western Australia and provided
much of the sustenance for the main
settlement on the Swan River. The town of
York, 95 kilometres east of Perth, reflects
the rustic solidarity of the region, the
produce of which ranges from fat lambs to
flour. However the Town Hall and Council
Chambers, completed in 1911, is in a style
totally foreign to its surroundings.

*Loop area in the Murchison
River, Western Australia*

*Hanks Head Lookout, Murchison River,
Western Australia*

Covering about 146 000 hectares, the
Kalbarri National Park consists mainly of
an elevated sand plain, split by a huge gorge
carved by the Murchison River through the
uptilted rim of the scarp. This spectacular
canyon is more than 80 kilometres long.
Its precipitous walls, in places brightly
stained by mineral leaching, are up to
152 metres high.

The stony Darling escarpment north of
Geraldton is split by Murchison River in a
series of wild, red-walled gorges which are
overpowering in the atmosphere of barren
savagery that hangs over them. This is
country for the nature lover who likes his
scenery raw and strongly flavoured. Only a
few kilometres away there are lush
wheatlands and a coast notable for its
gentle, pleasant contours.

*Sunset, Karri forest, Pemberton,
Western Australia*

The majestic Karri gums are the tallest
hardwood trees in Western Australia and
among the tallest growing in the southern
hemisphere. Apart from the splendour of
their appearance, the Karri trees are a
valuable source of timber for their straight
trunks can soar for 50 metres before
dividing into branches. The town of
Pemberton is surrounded for hundreds of
square kilometres by these forest giants.
This is a great milling district, providing
some of the best hardwood timbers.

*Porongorups Reservoir, south-western Western Australia*

*Water splashing over the weir, Pemberton, Western Australia*

Two notably beautiful mountain ranges rise from the western escarpment of the continent in the south-western corner of Western Australia. They are the Porongorups and the Stirling Range in the heart of the Karri forests for which the State is famous. The rainfall of this region averages between 1000 and 1500 millimetres a year and the countryside is green for most of the time.

Pemberton, town of the 'Kingdom of the Karri', is 340 kilometres south of Perth. The small sawmilling town is in a valley between hills covered with tall Karri eucalypts, where some of the best areas have been preserved in Warren National Park, Beedelup National Park, Carey Park, Brockway Forest and Big Brook Forest. The Lefroy Brook, tributary of the Warren River, flows through Pemberton.

*Falls and pool on the Serpentine River, Western Australia*

*Bushfire in the Karri forest, Western Australia*

The Serpentine River rises in the Darling Range south-east of Perth and flows north-west to the Serpentine Falls. These falls are augmented by drainage channels from Large Eye, Small Eye and Magenup Swamps. Pipeline Dam, upstream of the falls, is the first stage of the Serpentine Dam project, designed to supplement the Perth metropolitan water supply.

Fires—mostly caused by human agency—sweep through the heavily timbered country south of Perth with tragic regularity. They are incredibly destructive but have their moments of melancholy beauty as this study of a sorely wounded forest shows.

*Next pages: State Hotel, Gwalia, Western Australia*

*Wesley Church ruins, Greenough, Western Australia*

*Kwinana Freeway at night, Perth, Western Australia*

Greenough, situated near the mouth of the Greenough River about 480 kilometres north of Perth, was once an important wheat-yielding district. However, rust frequently ruined the crops and disastrous floods late in the 1880s finally brought the district's wheat industry to its knees. Many picturesque ruins of mills, barns and churches remain as stark reminders of nature's opposition to man's intrusion.

A modern highway with a sleek new bridge across the Swan River near its estuary at Fremantle now connects Perth with Kwinana, a complex of heavy industrial plants which has grown up on the shores of Cockburn Sound over the last 20 years. The lights of the bridge and the highway are strikingly beautiful on a summer night.

**Mounts Toolbrunup and Hassell,
Stirling Range, Western Australia**

**Fish-hook Bay, Rottnest Island,
Western Australia**

A drive through the Stirling Range provides many scenes like this of huge fists of rock thrusting up from the surface of the earth. Although not as high as Bluff Knoll, Mount Toolbrunup reaches 1052 metres, and the height of these rocky projections is emphasised by the flatness of the surrounding countryside. Most visitors to this range are impressed by the spectacular carpet of spring wildflowers.

A few kilometres off the coast of Western Australia is Perth's holiday island of Rottnest — a low-lying island which offers the simple attractions of sun, sand and a rich marine and land life. The early Dutch navigators who named the island mistook its population of rare quokka wallabies for giant rats — hence the name, which means 'rats' nest'. Rottnest is only 19 kilometres from Fremantle.

# In the tropics
## From grasslands to the Great Barrier Reef

From Cape York to the Kimberleys the far north of Australia has far more geographical and climatic unity than a quick glance at a political map might suggest.

Much of the continent lies in the tropics, north of the Tropic of Capricorn. Parts of the Kimberleys of Western Australia therefore have much in common with the top end of the Northern Territory and the Cape York Peninsula of Queensland; certainly more than they do with the temperate country in the south-west of their own state of Western Australia.

The far north is country where the gently merging seasons of spring, summer, autumn and winter are replaced by just two, 'the wet' and 'the dry'.

'The wet' comes with the monsoons, and lasts from December to April. It is a time of pounding rain, devastating floods and destructive cyclones, a time when much outdoor activity has to be abandoned, when travel from place to place, even by air, can become impossible.

In the Queensland section of the far north, the general structure of eastern Australia persists, with north-south arrangements of the coast, the coastal plain, the Great Dividing Range, and the country beyond it.

But there is a new feature here, an extra north-south factor, the Great Barrier Reef. The greatest structure ever built by living creatures, the coral polyps, the reef is more like a geological phenomenon, more like rock than bone. It stretches for 2000 kilometres along much of the east coast of Queensland, and stands anywhere between 15 and 250 kilometres out to sea.

Further north, the Gulf of Carpentaria, 450 kilometres from east to west, and 650 kilometres from north to south, bites deeply into Australia's northern coast. On both its eastern and western shores nature has provided some of the world's most extensive deposits of bauxite, the precious red dirt that is the raw material for one of the twentieth century's most sought after metals, aluminium.

Sitting astride the imaginary line that separates Queensland from the Northern Territory, the Barkly Tableland is an area of undulating, well-grassed country ideal for cattle. Here are to be found those enormous cattle stations that are as big as some European countries, stations such as Alexandria, the biggest in Australia, and the famous Brunette Downs.

To Western Australians the far north means the Kimberleys and the Pilbara, the two areas north of the 26th parallel of south latitude.

The Kimberleys, roughly the area north of Roebuck Bay and the old pearling port of Broome, have been called 'brutally beautiful'. The Kimberley rivers carry enormous volumes of water during 'the wet' and people have started to tame them with such projects as the Ord River scheme designed to bring dry-season water to cotton and other crops on the black soil plains of the East Kimberleys.

South of the Kimberleys lies the Pilbara, a land of red mountains that proved to be among the richest iron ore deposits in the world. The rainfall is lower here, and the rivers that thread their way through this iron land are usually dry and sandy, and lined by white gums, with the occasional permanent pool captured within rocky bars. It was near one of these bars that Marble Bar, reputedly Australia's hottest town, grew up in the days of an earlier mining age, when men came to the Pilbara not for iron but for gold.

*Giant figtree, Atherton Tableland, Queensland*

Long Island Sound from Humpty Point, Queensland

Sands of Sarina Inlet,
central Queensland coast

Gorge in Hamersley Ranges, near
Wittenoom, Western Australia

The sun-drenched sands of Sarina Inlet lie just south of Mackay on the central Queensland coast. The inlet is fringed by lush tropical vegetation produced by an annual 1772 millimetre rainfall which also assists the growing of sugar cane around the town of Sarina. Back in 1927, the little settlement of Sarina boasted Australia's first power alcohol distillery; today it offers superb facilities for the tourist.

Stretching for nearly 500 kilometres across the arid Pilbara division of the far north-west, the Hamersleys are noted for the wide variety of colours reflected from their rocks; rich red, violet and deep brown are typical. They are especially intense after rain has washed away the powdery ironstone dust which normally covers them. The entire region is highly mineralized, with many mountains composed of high grade iron ore.

*Picturesque Clifton Beach,
northern Queensland coast*

*Pentecost Island, Whitsunday
Passage, Queensland*

Wedged between Palm Cove to the north
and Trinity Beach to the south, Clifton
Beach epitomises all the qualities expected
of a northern Australian beach — a long
expanse of warm, golden sand fringed by
lush tropical forest and azure sea.

Lying north of Lindeman Island, the small
Pentecost Island shares the same azure seas
and balmy climate as the numerous other
famed island resorts of the Whitsunday
Passage. It is distinguishable by a sheer,
rocky cliff face which rises spectacularly
from the sea at the north-eastern end.

*Loggerhead Turtle, Great Barrier Reef, Queensland*

*Coral of the Great Barrier Reef, Queensland*

This long-necked variety of turtle is not as common as the Green Turtle in Australian waters but it occurs in large numbers on the Great Barrier Reef. Like all sea turtles it lays a clutch of eggs in a hole high up on the beach, covers it with sand and abandons the young to hatch out and make the perilous journey unassisted down the sand to the water.

This 2012 kilometres long series of reefs is the largest coral conglomeration in the world, with many varieties of spectacularly beautiful coral, mostly submerged. The tiny coral-making creatures, called polyps, form colonies of different sizes, shapes and colours according to their species. About 350 kinds of coral have now been identified on the Barrier Reef — some of a soft, gelatinous texture, others hard and spiny.

*Victoria River Crossing landscape, Northern Territory*

With the Daly River, the Victoria River is the most important stream of water in the Northern Territory. It was first crossed by Alexander Forrest when he was exploring the area in 1879. The famous Victoria River Downs was the first cattle station to be established on the river in 1883. The Victoria wanders over the Northern Territory countryside for 644 kilometres before entering Joseph Bonaparte Gulf on the northern coast near the border of Western Australia. The white gums and reddish-pink colour of the river cliffs are typical of the landscape in much of the semi-arid regions of the north.

*Coastal scene, Port Douglas,*
*northern Queensland*

*The Esplanade, Cairns,*
*northern Queensland*

Founded in 1876 when Christie Palmerston discovered a shorter route to the Palmer Goldfields, Port Douglas was the chief town of northern Queensland until 1886 when the gold ran out. From that time, trade was lost to the railhead at Cairns and today the town functions only as a seaport for the sugarlands of Mossman and the surrounding district.

Cairns, the most northerly city in Queensland, is a pleasant palm- and garden-studded city on Trinity Bay, with broad streets and buildings that are shaded against the tropical sun. It is the tourist centre of the north; an ideal staging point for visits to Barrier Reef islands, the surroundng scenic areas and the tablelands. For the intrepid, there is the harsh and wild country of the Cape York Peninsula.

*Jedda Rock, Katherine Gorge,*
*Northern Territory*

*Giant anthills, desert country,*
*Northern Territory*

The town of Katherine, about 320 kilometres south of Darwin, draws its prosperity from the surrounding cattle stations, an abattoir and, more recently, from tourism. About 30 kilometres from the town is the Katherine Gorge where the river flows, clean and swift, between towering canyon walls. Jedda Rock takes its name from the Charles Chauvel movie *Jedda,* which was filmed in the area.

Colonies of white ants or, more accurately, termites construct these extraordinary mounds of digested mud which are a feature of northern landscapes, particularly in the Northern Territory and the Kimberleys. The hills may be three to five metres high and contain a labyrinth of galleries in which the creatures store food and shelter from the heat. Hectares of flat, dry country are covered by these bizarre structures.

Townsville from Magnetic Island, Queensland

*Fitzroy Bridge and River, Rockhampton,
central Queensland*

*Entrance to Trinity Bay, Cairns,
northern Queensland*

The major city of Queensland's central
coastal region, Rockhampton is the centre
of a web of main roads, railways and air
routes from the coast to the grainlands and
pastures of the west. From its beginnings
Rockhampton was seen as the future capital
of the north and its architectural heritage
today enhances a thriving, modern city of
gardens and plantations of tropical trees
and shrubs.

Cairns is built on the coast and overlooks
the natural harbour of Trinity Bay.
Equipped with bulk sugar loading facilities,
its port channels the rich harvest of the
hinterland to export markets. The coastal
strip, bounded by the ocean on one side
and rainforest on the other, is criss-crossed
by orderly farmland producing sugar,
tobacco, timber, maize, peanuts, fruit and
dairy cattle.

Heron Island, a coral cay,
central Queensland coast

Pentecost Island from Lindeman Island,
central Queensland coast

In the Capricorn Group of islands, 80 kilometres out from Gladstone on the Queensland coast lies Heron Island, a flat coral cay of about 16 hectares. Most of this area is a National Park; the remainder supports a thriving tourist trade. The island is formed of coral reefs and sand and rises no more than 2.5 metres above the sand, but it is covered by 12-metre high Pisonia forest and groves of Pandanus.

The Whitsunday and Lindeman Groups, off the coast from Proserpine on the central Queensland coast, are amongst Australia's most well-known and scenically beautiful islands and, collectively, provide one of Queensland's greatest tourist potentials. Pentecost Island, on part of the world-famous Great Barrier Reef, is dominated by nearby Lindeman Island.

*South Molle and North Molle Islands,
North Queensland*

*Pioneer River Valley from Eungella,
Queensland*

Both are small, sparsely timbered, rocky islets east of Shute Harbour north of Mackay. The larger, South Molle is about four kilometres long and two and a half kilometres wide and rises to an altitude of 210 metres. The soil is unusually fertile and the tourist centre, served by helicopter, aircraft and launches from Proserpine on the mainland, runs a fruit and vegetable farm to supply its restaurants.

Tall palms and abundant undergrowth typify the vegetation of this area. The Pioneer River drains Eungella National Park, the largest mountain reserve in Queensland, and magnificent views can be gained from vantage points on a scenic road which crosses the valley. The Pioneer River was originally called the Mackay after John Mackay who discovered the valley in 1860.

*Colonial residence, Townsville, northern Queensland*

The fierce tropical climate of northern Queensland brought a sensible, and at times graceful, response from architects. This stately weatherboard residence at Townsville is in the classic vernacular style of the early northern homestead, with stilts to create a breezeway and deep verandahs.

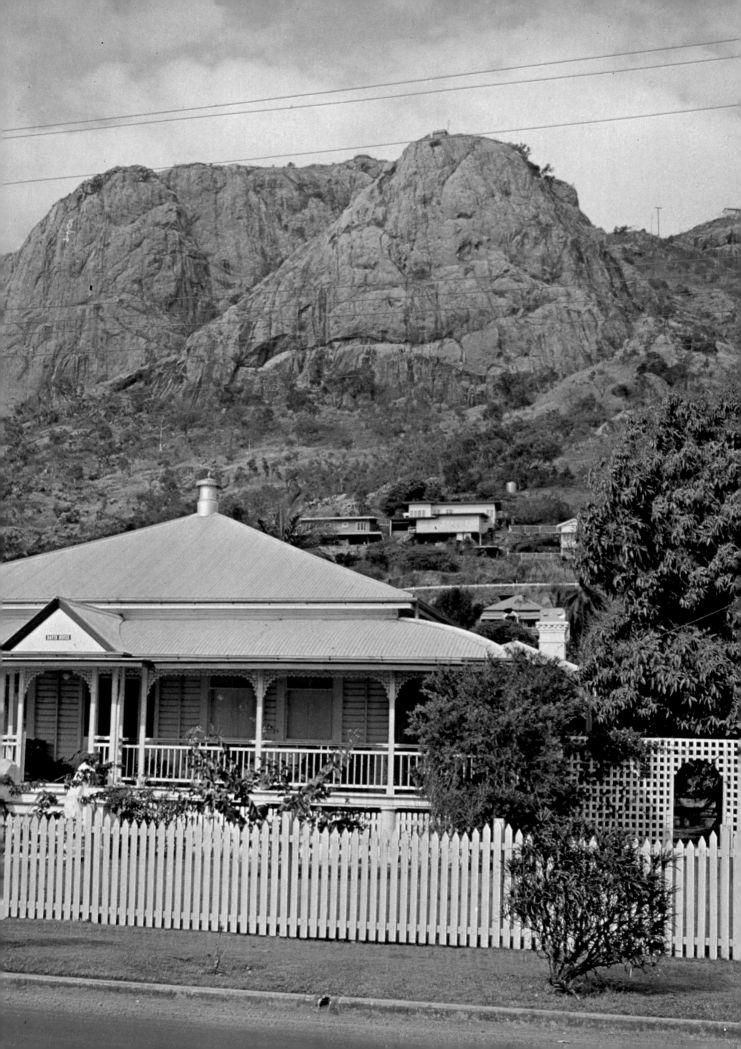

*Glen Allyn Falls, Atherton,*
*northern Queensland*

*Trinity Beach coastline near Cairns,*
*northern Queensland*

The heavy rain which falls on the scenic Atherton Tableland creates a landscape of tumbling water and verdant, jungle-like forests. John Atherton was the first pastoralist to capitalize on this region's combination of bounteous rainfall and rich, volcanic soil; today, the area around Atherton has been cleared to produce fine crops of maize and peanuts as well as supporting dairying, pigs and timber.

Trinity Bay provides the coastal city of Cairns with a magnificent natural harbour. During World War Two this harbour was of great importance and oil tanks and a wharf were built for refuelling supply ships. However, war is far from the minds of the tourists who lie on the sun-warmed sand of one of the beautiful beaches of the area. These include Clifton, Machan's or Trinity Beaches which all lie north of Cairns.

117

*Aerial view of cane fields,
southern Queensland*

*The Pinnacle, Cape Hillsborough,
central Queensland*

Queensland's sugar industry began with
Captain Louis Hope's successful
establishment of a plantation near Brisbane
in 1862; the 'Sunshine State' now produces
the majority of Australia's sugar. The cane
is grown on about 10 000 plantations
averaging 28 hectares. When the crops are
mature, the leaves are burned off to
facilitate the operation of giant mechanical
harvesters.

Cape Hillsborough National Park, 45
kilometres north of Mackay, is a tropical
wonderland of caves, hills and rugged
seashores made accessible to the visitor by
carefully graded bush tracks with extensive
picnic and camping areas. One rocky
outcrop has been aptly named The Pinnacle
and rises abruptly and dramatically above
its park-like surroundings.

*Lamington National Park,*
*southern Queensland*

*Figtree landscape, Cooktown area,*
*northern Queensland*

Behind the Gold Coast, and giving it a scenic dimension, lies Mount Lamington National Park in the MacPherson Range. This area contains some of the most beautiful mountain and rainforest country in Australia, and is a haven for those who want to escape from the pace of life below. The MacPherson Range rises to an altitude of more than 1219 metres and is covered by thick sub-tropical forests.

Forest giants like this one are common in the impenetrable rainforests of northern Queensland, but become striking landmarks when left as solitary, majestic survivors of land clearance.

120

*Russell River and Mount Bartle Frere,
northern Queensland*

South of Cairns the Russell and the
Mulgrave rivers flow together amidst a tangle
of jungle, providing an ideal habitat for
saltwater crocodiles. Visitors may cruise
these waters and see vistas of jungle ferns,
palms and brightly-coloured flowers with
the summit of Bartle Frere, the state's
tallest peak, dominating the background.
Rising more than 1500 metres above the
surrounding countryside, this mountain
often seems moody and mysterious with its
head shrouded in mist and its slopes
clothed in thick, moist vegetation.

*Bushy Cay and atoll,
northern Queensland coast*

*Idyllic sweep of coastline, Cannonvale,
northern Queensland*

Numerous cays and atolls have formed over
a great many years within the huge precinct
of the Great Barrier Reef. Although both
arise on coral reefs and are principally
made of coral, they differ in appearance;
a cay is a small island whereas an atoll is a
ring-shaped coral reef enclosing a lagoon.
On some cays there has been a build up of
crushed coral and sand sufficient to support
some small patches of vegetation.

On the way from Proserpine to Shute
Harbour, take-off point for the islands of
the Great Barrier Reef, the traveller passes
through Cannonvale. It is a small community
which clusters along an attractive beach
front offering ideal facilities for fishing and
shelling — with a magnificent backdrop of
islands and deep blue-green sea.

*The bridge at Innisfail, northern Queensland coast*

*Johnstone River, Innisfail, northern Queensland*

Some 90 kilometres south of Cairns, Innisfail is set at the confluence of the North and South Johnstone Rivers. Like its neighbouring cities, Innisfail has gained prosperity through sugar production — an industry now rivalled by tourism as more and more people are pushing northwards along the Bruce Highway to enjoy the sun-drenched seclusion of the beautiful beaches and the northern tropical towns.

The area around the Johnstone River was opened up by the exploration of George Dalrymple in 1873 and eight years later the first sugar mill was built. Since then, during the months of June to December, the population of Innisfail swells with the seasonal influx of cane-cutters. At nearby Mourilyan Harbour bulk sugar terminals house the huge quantities of crushed sugar produced in the region.

# The south-east

## A landscape moulded by mountain and stream

Look at a relief map of Australia and you could think that some enormous force had shaken the continent until most of its great mountains and great rivers had tumbled into the south-east corner.

Australia's Southern Alps, or Snowy Mountains, are part of the Great Dividing Range, that spinal column of mountains that runs right down the east coast of the continent.

They give rise to such rivers as the Snowy, Murray, Tumut and Murrumbidgee. The Snowy, which once poured its waters coastwards into the Tasman Sea, now flows inland through man-made tunnels and man-made lakes to generate electricity and to add its water to the Murray and Murrumbidgee for inland irrigation.

Two other mountain systems help define the land forms of Australia's south-east: the Grampians of Western Victoria and the Lofty Ranges-Flinders Ranges group of South Australia.

Taken together with the Snowy Mountains, they form the bowl that provides the northern and north-eastern slopes of Victoria, the Wimmera of Victoria, the Mallee of Victoria and South Australia and the Riverina of New South Wales.

It was there that Thomas Livingstone Mitchell in 1836 found 'open grassy plains, beautifully variegated with serpentine lines of wood' and country 'shining fresh and green in the light of a fine morning'.

But the settlers that followed found much of this area dry and less inviting to human habitation than Mitchell thought. Rainfall is light and the rivers rush through it in an annual surge as the spring and summer sun melts the snow on the Snowy Mountains. But the area has not been left

*Left: Russell Falls, Mount Field, southern Tasmania*

to its own inclinations and a series of irrigation schemes has converted much of it into a patchwork of orchards, vineyards, ricefields and pastures.

South of the mountains, the country falls into two fairly distinct areas, both in the path of rain-bearing winds that have travelled the Great Australian Bight. To the east is Gippsland, a rugged and well-watered region that explorer Angus McMillan in 1840 named Caledonia Australis, the Scotland of the South. In earlier days it was a vast forest, as present day deposits of brown coal and offshore oil attest. To the west is the grassy plain of South Australia's south-east and Victoria's Western District, one natural unit divided in two by a line drawn on a map by public servants sitting in an office in London in the 1830s. In a continent famous for its wool, nowhere is more renowned than this area.

The south-east has some of Australia's most rugged coast, washed by some of its wildest seas. It is at its most spectacular at such places as the Twelve Apostles and London Bridge on the western coast of Victoria, and Cape Raoul in Tasmania, at its most serene at places like the Ninety Mile Beach in Victoria. Deep indents such as St Vincent Gulf, Port Phillip Bay and Westernport Bay provide the major cities of the area, Adelaide, Geelong and Melbourne, with long stretches of coastal playgrounds.

To most people, Australia's island state of Tasmania is either the Isle of Mountains or the Apple Isle, depending on whether they prefer their landscapes rugged and untamed, or orderly and productive.

The combination of high land and high rainfall makes Tasmania ideal hydro-electricity country, and dams, pipelines and powerhouses have become part of the state's landscape.

Taroona and Derwent landscape,
southern Tasmania

*Coles Bay and The Hazards,*
*Freycinet Peninsula, Tasmania*

*Cloudy Bay, South Bruny Island,*
*southern Tasmania*

Tasmania's national parks and reserves encompass spectacular peaks and lakes, dense forest lands and rugged coasts. The largest of the coastal reserves is the Freycinet National Park which flanks the picturesque Coles Bay at the north-west of the Freycinet Peninsula. This is a region of secluded coves and sunny beaches, rock pools and bush tracks lined with wildflowers in spring.

Cloudy Bay on the south-east coast of the mountainous South Bruny Island offers superb coastal scenery. On the other side of the island, on historic Adventure Bay, is Fluted Cape, a high striated cliff face where the hills of South Bruny meet the sea. The Fluted Cape-Cloudy Bay region is a coastal reserve and is adjacent to another reserve at Waterfall Creek. Access to Bruny Island is by ferry from Kettering south of Hobart.

*Autumnal landscape in the Tumut
Valley, New South Wales*

*Autumn foliage on the Tumut
River, New South Wales*

The township of Tumut stands 32
kilometres from the Hume Highway.
Although it is a small manufacturing
centre, mainly processing primary products,
it is better-known to the traveller for its
many fine stands of introduced trees and
the splendid displays of foliage they
provide as autumn approaches. Every May
the annual event is celebrated in the
Falling Leaves festival.

Magnificent displays of autumn foliage
occur on the Tumut River near the town of
Tumut, the northern gateway to the
Kosciusko State Park. The Tumut area is
brought to a point of fine grandeur in the
autumn when the magnificent stands of
European trees show their best.

*Next pages: Autumnal avenue near
Longford, northern Tasmania*

*Hop-picking time, Ellendale, southern Tasmania*

*Remains of the church, Port Arthur, Tasmania*

The Derwent Valley, north-west of Hobart, is the centre of Tasmania's hop-growing industry, which supplies breweries throughout Australia. The valley is particularly beautiful in autumn when the hops are being harvested and when the introduced English trees, predominantly poplars, willows and myrtles, are turning to gold.

The ruins of the stone church are set in parkland near the shore at Port Arthur on the south-eastern coast. Said to have been designed by convict James Blackburn, the church was built from richly-hued local sandstone between 1836 and 1841. The church had thirteen spires, representing Christ and the apostles, and seated a congregation of 1200, more than 1000 of whom were convicts.

*Wilsons Promontory, from
Mount Oberon, Victoria*

*Apple blossoms, Huon Valley,
southern Tasmania*

A wild, desolate headland thrusting deep
into the waters of Bass Strait, Wilsons
Promontory has been reserved as a national
park and sanctuary since 1908. Its highest
point is Mount Latrobe, 740 metres above
sea-level, which like many other peaks on
its rocky spine, commands breathtaking
views of coast and heathland; and of the
tea-tree and lillipilli forests which flourish
in the more sheltered valleys.

The Huon River Valley and the Huon
Peninsula, just south of Hobart, is the most
famous apple-growing district in Australia
and is a scenic delight as the thousands of
hectares of apple orchards burst with
blooms in the soft spring sunshine. Many of
the orchards are more than a century old,
and the industry is said to have begun
under the encouragement of Lady Franklin,
the wife of a Governor of Tasmania.

*Hobart, from Mount Wellington peak, Tasmania*

*Constitution Dock, Derwent River, Hobart, Tasmania*

Perhaps the most beautifully sited of Australia's major cities, Hobart is flanked by the broad estuary of the Derwent River and overlooked by the forested and often snow-capped Mount Wellington. Founded in 1804 by Lieutenant Governor David Collins, Hobart grew quickly to a busy seaport for whalers and timber ships. Even today, the romantic colonial character of Tasmania's capital is retained.

The island state's capital is strongly maritime in character; its fine deep-water port has felt the pulse of the city's life since early days. Its wharves, once home of the bond stores and warehouses of the old merchants, now accommodate passenger and cargo liners from all over the world.

*Over page: Convict-built bridge at Ross*

143

*Mount Roland, Great Western Tiers,
northern Tasmania*

*Quelltaler Vineyards and Winery,
Watervale, South Australia*

On the southern edge of the fertile coastal
belt of northern Tasmania rises the densely-
forested mountain barrier known as the
Great Western Tiers. From the sea, this
range resembles an unbroken wall but in
reality some parts of this fault-escarpment,
like Quamby Bluff or Mount Roland, are
higher or detached from the main line.
Beyond lies the Central Plateau, like a
table-top sloping gently to the south.

Watervale, north of Adelaide, in the North
Mount Lofty Ranges, supports thriving
vineyards. John Macarthur planted
Australia's first vineyard at Camden, New
South Wales, in 1820 and since then
Australia has gradually built up a fine wine
industry. In South Australia planting began
in the 1840s and within a short time
vineyards at Morphett Vale, Yalumba,
Seppeltsfield and Auldana were flourishing.

*The Gulch, Bicheno fishing port, Tasmania*

*Dove Lake and Cradle Mountain, Lake St Clair National Park, Tasmania*

The east coast of Tasmania is reminiscent of the mainland coast: picturesque rather than spectacular. Its seaside towns, many on sheltered inlets, are popular with holiday makers and it has excellent surf beaches and fishing and boating water. Bicheno, 170 kilometres south-east of Launceston, is typical of the charming resorts the area offers.

Cradle Mountain is so named because it holds the Dove and Crater lakes in a high-altitude cradle of volcanic stone. The mountain, 1577 metres high, is one among giants in this wild region of open moorland and heaths, deep gorges and forested valleys sprinkled with lakes and tarns. The main bushwalking track begins at Waldheim Chalet, where there is a museum devoted to the flora, fauna and geology of the region.

*Rugged western Grampians Range, western Victoria*

*Mount Buffalo road approach, Australian Alps, Victoria*

Discovered and named by Thomas Mitchell in 1836, the Grampians are the 'tail end' of the Great Dividing Range and run north-south for approximately 96 kilometres from Glenorchy to Dunkeld in western Victoria. This wild, bold and austere mountain range rises in sharp contrast to the surrounding plains and is composed of sandstone and granite which have been worn away by wind and water.

Mount Buffalo, in the Australian Alps, is one of the favourite resorts of Victorian snow-seekers. The 1721 metre peak rises above the isolated granite plateau of the Mount Buffalo National Park, 322 kilometres north-east of Melbourne, and is strewn with many tors and granite blocks, including a number of great balanced boulders. The Buffalo Gorge is one of the features of the mountain.

*Mount Feathertop from Hotham skifields, Victoria*

In winter the highest mountains in the Australian Alps present scenes of breathtaking beauty. Mount Feathertop, reaching a height of 1922 metres is the giant of the Victorian Alps. Although nearly bare of trees at the higher levels, it stands surrounded by precipitous, heavily-timbered country in a labyrinth of mountains and valleys. Snow usually covers the peak in autumn and remains until early summer. Although it provides excellent open skiing conditions, the peak has not been developed as a skiing resort, unlike Mount Hotham (foreground), 8 kilometres to the south.

152

*'Coonawarra' on Murray River near Swan Reach, South Australia*

*Exhibition Buildings, Carlton Gardens, Melbourne, Victoria*

The 'Coonawarra' (the name means 'Black Swan' in one of the Aboriginal tongues) has its base at Murray Bridge in South Australia and has for several years been navigating the Murray between Murray Bridge and Morgan on five-day cruises. At first glance, the vessel looks like the paddle-steamers that carried wool and timber on the river 100 years ago, but diesel engines have replaced the old smoke-belching steam engines.

Second city of Australia and capital of Victoria, Melbourne is a metropolis of architectural inconsistencies, yet it has dignity and beauty conferred by wide, tree-lined streets and spacious public gardens. The Exhibition Buildings, constructed to house the great Exhibition of 1880, provided the venue for the first Australian Parliament, opened in 1901 by the Duke of York.

*Cloudy Bay Lagoon, South Bruny Island, Tasmania*

*Mount Townsend, Snowy Mountains, New South Wales*

Beauty and serenity reign at Cloudy Bay lagoon at South Bruny Island — one of the world's quieter places. The 221-square-kilometre island is long and irregularly shaped and shelters much of the Huon Valley coast. It is mountainous in the south, well wooded and picturesque, with a rugged east coast facing the ocean and a number of enclosed bays to shelter small craft.

These gorge-cleft highlands clothed in sombre forests are the great rain trap in which the Murray-Murrumbidgee river system has its source. An elaborate series of dams at lower levels harnesses the water-power to generate electricity for the major cities of Sydney and Melbourne and feeds the canals of the Riverina irrigation system which contributes much to the rural wealth of the nation.

*Richmond Bridge, Richmond, southern Tasmania*

*Ruins of the Port Arthur Penal Settlement, southern Tasmania*

This beautiful freestone bridge about 25 kilometres from Hobart on the road to Port Arthur was designed by David Lambe and built by convicts in 1823. It is the oldest structure of its kind still in use in Australia. Local stone quarried at Butcher's Hill was used, but formidable engineering problems—the river floods violently—raised the cost of construction to £20 000, an almost astronomical figure in those days.

Between 1830 and 1877 some 10 000 convicts, including children, were transported to Tasmania (then known as Van Diemen's Land) to serve their terms. Many did not survive to live as free men. Today, the ruins of the Port Arthur Penal Settlement are visited by thousands of people annually.

*Reflections in the waters of
Lake Pedder, Tasmania*

*Tamar River near Launceston,
northern Tasmania*

*Narcissus River, Lake St Clair
National Park, Tasmania*

This 64 kilometre tidal estuary, formed at Launceston by the junction of the North and South Esk Rivers, flows north-west through wool and fat lamb country to Port Dalrymple. Sited on the banks of the Tamar, Launceston is the air, sea and rail centre for northern Tasmania and main port for Bass Strait shipping. It was first settled in 1806, officially became a town in 1824 and a city in 1888.

The Narcissus River flows through the Cradle Mountain-Lake St Clair National Park. This is the second largest park in Tasmania and a major wild-life sanctuary and scenic reserve. The park covers 1360 square kilometres of rugged mountain peaks, deep valleys and alpine moors. An 84 kilometre track between Cradle Mountain and Lake St Clair is a mecca for bushwalkers.

*The Devil's Kitchen, Tasman
Peninsula, Tasmania*

*Rocky coastline at Eaglehawk
Neck, Tasmania*

The Devil's Kitchen is one of a fascinating aggregation of geological features near Eaglehawk Neck on the Tasman Peninsula's seaward coastline. It is an impressive coastline of towering cliffs and capes, often weathered into strange shapes by the pounding of the ocean. Other features near the Devil's Kitchen are the Tessellated Pavement, the Blowhole and Tasman's Arch.

The cliffs of Eaglehawk Neck on the Tasman Peninsula presented a landscape to make the convict's heart quail. This narrow strip of land connects the peninsula—on which was sited the Port Arthur prison and penal settlement—with the rest of the island. It thus served as an effective natural barrier to the escape of convicts. Dogs were chained across the peninsula to apprehend escapees, and the line was patrolled by guards.

*Aerial view of Adelaide and Torrens River, South Australia*

*Batman Bridge, Tamar River, Tasmania*

South Australia's capital is built on the narrow coastal plain between the Gulf of St Vincent and the abruptly rising Mount Lofty Range which commands striking panoramas of the city. Adelaide is orderly and culture-conscious; the Adelaide Festival of Arts, held every two years, has become an important part of Australian theatrical life and draws people from many parts of the world to this handsome city.

The wide Tamar River runs 48 kilometres from the northern Tasmanian coast to join the North Esk and South Esk rivers at Launceston. The Tamar is a picturesque tidal estuary with many fine fishing reaches and attractive beaches at its seaward end. It is flanked by two highways which are linked by the Batman Bridge near the heads, enabling motorists to make a 100-kilometre round trip.

Historic Entally House, near Launceston,
northern Tasmania

*Mount Abrupt, the Grampians,
western Victoria*

*Dragon's Jaws in the Grampians,
western Victoria*

The Grampians of western Victoria have their own style of rugged beauty. Although the highest peak reaches only 1167 metres, the steepness and isolation of these mountains make them appear much higher than they really are. From a distance, the range contrasts strongly with the predominant colouring of the plains from which they rise.

In the Grampians, great tilted slabs of sandstone have been shaped by the elements into weird forms which project upwards or hang precariously over deep valleys. This uniquely beautiful mountain range lies in the general shape of a boomerang and many visitors are attracted here by the spring wildflowers and by such fascinating rock formations as the Grand Canyon, Great Stairway and Dragon's Jaws.

*Historic Penny Royal watermill,*
*Launceston, Tasmania*

*Gunn's Plains landscape,*
*northern Tasmania*

The city of Launceston has many fascinating places and buildings of historic interest, such as the rustic stone Penny Royal watermill. The building was restored in colonial style for use as a restaurant. The city is at the junction of three rivers—the Tamar, the North Esk and the South Esk. Another of its water features is the Cataract Gorge on the South Esk River. The rapids in the canyon are most spectacular after rain.

One of the richest and most picturesque farming regions in northern Tasmania is Gunn's Plains, which spreads through the narrow valley of the Leven River and is surrounded by thickly wooded hills. At various points on the inland roads from coastal Penguin and Ulverstone there are superb panoramic views of the valley and the winding river.

Adelong landscape, near the Tumut
River, New South Wales

*Cook Rivulet, Adventure Bay,*
*South Bruny Island, Tasmania*

*Salvation Jane in flower, Flinders*
*Ranges, South Australia*

Historic associations ring clear in the place names and features of Bruny Island. The Cook Rivulet at Adventure Bay was named as a reminder of Captain James Cook's landing there in 1777. Adventure Bay was discovered by Captain Tobias Furneaux, second in command to Cook's second Pacific expedition. Captain William Bligh of the *Bounty* planted Tasmania's first apple trees there in 1788.

One of the most spectacular of the dry country ephemerals below the tropics, this plant—regarded as a noxious weed in other states because it is poisonous to stock— makes a brilliant display on the parklike savannahs of the Flinders Ranges. In different seasonal conditions the same slopes may be blanketed with wild hops, pink parakeelya or golden everlastings.

Peaks of Mount Lyell, western
coast, Tasmania

Queenstown and West Coast Range,
Tasmania

Rarely indeed is a man-made desert
beautiful, but there is a haunting grandeur
in these fantastic bare mountains near
Queenstown, a copper mining centre on
Tasmania's lonely west coast. Timber-getters
stripped the hills of trees to feed the
furnaces of the smelters, and chemical
fumes from their stacks killed off any
undergrowth remaining. The extraordinary
colours derive from mineral leaching.

Queenstown, with a population of around
5000 people, is the only sizeable settlement
on the wild west coast region. The town
depends for its existence on the fortunes
of the Mount Lyell copper plant, which
has operated since 1896, producing silver,
gold and copper. The great open cut for
the copper mining operation at West Lyell
is more than 1200 metres long, 600 metres
wide and 200 metres deep.

Old oast houses at Bushy
Park, Tasmania

# Red landscape

## The great plateau at the continent's centre

Take away Australia's tropical far north, sub-tropical east, the comparatively temperate south-east and south-west and what you have left is the red centre, the vast red inland plateau that occupies most of the continent. In places, such as along the shores of the Great Australian Bight, it reaches right to the coast.

The red centre is not without its spectacular landmarks, although much of it is monotonously flat.

Ayers Rock, one of its best-known visual symbols, a great red monolith, stands almost 350 metres above the surrounding plain. Its sides rise so abruptly that you can stand on level ground and rest your hands upon precipices that rise hundreds of metres above your head.

There are mountain ranges, too, to break the flatness, such as the MacDonnell and Musgrave Ranges of the true centre, around Alice Springs, made famous by Aboriginal artists of the Namatjira school, and the Flinders Ranges of South Australia, which white Australian artist Hans Heysen described as 'the bones of nature laid bare'.

On the other hand, Lake Eyre sinks into the plain, largest of the great salt lakes of inland Australia, lakes that only rarely contain water, but are for the most of the time vast wastes of saline mud. The rainfall rate around Lake Eyre is only 100 millimetres a year but the evaporation rate is 2500 millimetres.

Lake Eyre is about 12 metres below sea level, and the lowest spot in Australia, so it is the natural centre of the drainage system of much of the red centre. But while a number of streams flow towards it, most of them peter out before they ever reach it.

*Left: Stalactites, Ayers Rock cave, Northern Territory*

This happens in the Channel Country of south-west Queensland, the north-west of New South Wales and the north-east of South Australia. Here the main 'streams' are the Georgina River, the Diamantina River and the stream which even though it is formed by the junction of two rivers (the Thomson and the Barcoo) is known as Cooper Creek.

At times when the rains have been good these rivers spread themselves across 80 to 120 kilometre expanses of channels and produce such growth that they have been described as 'the world's only example of a vast irrigation scheme created by nature'. But only rarely do the waters come down in sufficient volume to reach Lake Eyre.

A landmark of a different kind is the completely treeless Nullarbor Plain, the arid, almost uninhabited limestone plateau that spreads across the border between south and western Australia. It begins with sheer cliffs that rise 100 metres out of the Great Australian Bight and runs north for 250 kilometres east and west for 650 kilometres.

The red centre is far from the dead heart, as it was sometimes called. Nature has evolved plants and animals to suit the arid climate, and even in the most unpromising areas experts can usually point to many signs of life.

Some plants of the red centre can exist for years, waiting for the occasional good rains to stimulate them into a frenzy of growth and renewal, bringing an almost parklike covering of green leaves and riotously coloured flowers.

Here and there the red centre becomes even less hospitable: in such places as the Simpson Desert, Sturt's Stony Desert, Great Victoria Desert, Gibson Desert, Great Sandy Desert, and Tanami Desert. Here even the sheep and cattle men have not penetrated.

*Entrance to the mighty Ormiston Gorge, Northern Territory*

*Ormiston Gorge and Mount Giles, Northern Territory*

Tourists have travelled from all over Australia to see the colours of the MacDonnell Ranges and to discover for themselves whether the watercolours of the Aboriginal artist, Albert Namatjira, are true to life; few are disappointed. Pink or red rocks, often with an underlying blue, give a colourful background to the rich browns and greens of the stately gums which grow only in those gorges where water is available.

The MacDonnell Ranges in central Australia run in several parallel ridges from east to west for about 322 kilometres, mostly to the west of Alice Springs. Although they rise for only about 300 to 450 metres above the surrounding plains, the MacDonnells exhibit an unusual amount of folding and there are dramatic gorges where rivers have cut a way through them.

184

*River Red Gums, Flinders Ranges, South Australia*

*Glen Helen Resort, Finke River, Northern Territory*

The Flinders Range presents some of the best mountain scenery in Australia. Matthew Flinders, after whom this range was named, first sighted the peaks in 1802. The Flinders are a continuation of the Mount Lofty Range which runs from near Adelaide to the head of the Spencer Gulf. Despite the aridity of the region, there is a surprising amount of vegetation. The giant River Red Gums are found along watercourses.

Deep in the MacDonnell Ranges, 136 kilometres west of Alice Springs lies the magnificent Glen Helen Gorge. Carved in prehistoric times by the waters of the Finke, the gorge is almost five kilometres long. At its northern end, the mighty bulk of Mount Sonder dominates the landscape beyond the Glen Helen tourist resort.

*Mount Conway area, MacDonnell
Ranges, Northern Territory*

*Standley Chasm, MacDonnell Ranges,
Northern Territory*

*Rock pools, Ormiston Pound,
Northern Territory*

Among the scenic attractions which draw
a multitude of tourists to the Centre each
year are the stark chasms and gorges cut
into the mountains by the Finke and other
rivers. The best-known of these spectacular
clefts lie to the west of the Alice. Within an
hour's drive, Heavitree Gap, Simpson's Gap
and Standley Chasm offer to the stranger
the first hint of the utter majesty of the
Centre.

The people of the Centre still face a harsh
and unforgiving land where water is a most
precious commodity. While maps reveal
rivers, creeks and lakes, in reality these are
often little more than series of unconnected
waterholes. Once great rivers coursed this
land but today it is a rare year indeed when
water flows the entire length of a river bed
and many streams run only after rain.

*Ayers Rock, landscape after rain,*
*Northern Territory*

*Rock reflections in Ormiston*
*Gorge, Northern Territory*

Dominating the skyline south-west of Alice Springs is Ayers Rock — 'Uluru' of Aboriginal legend, 'the Rock' to tourists. Tip of a buried sandstone range deposited some 500 to 600 million years ago, this startling monolith is 348 metres high and nine kilometres around. As the sun moves across the sky, so the rock changes colour and vivid oranges and pinks give way to purples and browns.

Although the vicissitudes of the last 500 million years have worn down the MacDonnells from a proud height of 4500 metres to a mere 300 metres, they have rewarded them with a unique character. Where else can one find sheer walls of red rock 60 metres high? Colour has been lavishly bestowed on the mountains of the MacDonnells, here mirrored in the waters of the Finke River.

*Mount Sonder, MacDonnell Ranges, Northern Territory*

*Standley Chasm, MacDonnell Ranges, Northern Territory*

Due west of Alice Springs, Mount Sonder is one of the giants of the Centre, rising to a height of 1330 metres above sea level. The rock of which it is formed is estimated to be 400 million years old. It is slashed by deep gorges and its original bedding planes have been so twisted by pressures in the earth's crust that they point vertically to the sky. Straggling lines of river gums indicate underground streams.

In Jay Creek Aboriginal Reserve some 70 kilometres west of Alice Springs, the MacDonnells are split by the awesome Standley Chasm. Here cliffs standing 60 to 75 metres high and only 3.5 to 5.5 metres apart change colour dramatically as the sun strikes the deep recesses. The chasm is named after Mrs Ida Standley, the first school-teacher in Alice Springs.

**Sand dunes of the Simpson Desert, Northern Territory**

**John Flynn Memorial, Mount Gillen Northern Territory**

This large area which seems to stretch to infinity is made up of arid sandhill and spinifex country. These ridges of red sand run in parallel lines right across the desert for about 161 kilometres. The Simpson Desert was first sighted by Charles Sturt in 1845 and it covers an area of 145 000 square kilometres. The colour and magnitude can only really be appreciated from the air.

Near Mount Gillen, a few kilometres west of Alice Springs, an eight-tonne boulder from the famous Devil's Marbles marks the grave of the Reverend John Flynn. 'Flynn of the Inland', a Presbyterian missionary, is best-remembered for his work as superintendent of the Australian Inland Mission. He was also deeply involved in the introduction of the Royal Flying Doctor Service and the Flying Ambulance.

*Gosse's Bluff landscape, Glen Helen, Northern Territory*

*Repeating fold formations, MacDonnell Ranges, Northern Territory*

To the south-west of Glen Helen, the mighty Gosse's Bluff resembles a landscape from a science-fiction thriller. Here a circle of ruined hills encloses a crater where a meteor is believed to have crashed to earth eons ago. The formation is named after the explorer W. C. Gosse who, in 1873, discovered Ayers Rock.

The MacDonnell Range system of central Australia marches in long and eerily symmetrical lines across the land. Hidden within the stark chains of rock are places which, although overshadowed by the magnificence of Ayers Rock and The Olgas, have their own fantastic beauty of shape, colour and texture. To the west of Alice Springs, the MacDonnells stretch away to the horizon in repeating fold formations.

St Mary's Peak, Flinders Ranges, South Australia

*Seemingly precarious Devil's Marbles, Northern Territory*

*Organ Pipes formation, Finke River, Northern Territory*

These extraordinary granite residuals are a famous landform straddling the Stuart Highway about 97 kilometres south of Tennant Creek. Hundreds of gigantic, rounded granite boulders, sometimes balanced on top of one another, are scattered in heaps which appear to have been hurled down by a giant hand. Granite often weathers into rounded shapes as exfoliation peels off layer after layer.

High sharp battlements known as the Organ Pipes are reflected in a waterhole on the Finke River. For much of the year the bed of the Finke is arid, dead; a mere ghost of what a river should be. But from time to time, after heavy rains, the river fills, often spilling over its banks, and rampages south to join the Macumba river and empty into Lake Eyre.

*Ayers Rock sunrise,*
*Northern Territory*

*Mount Olga group from the air,
Northern Territory*

*Head of King's Canyon,
Northern Territory*

The Olgas is the name given to this cluster of rounded massive rocks rising from the spinifex plain. They are as dramatic and vividly coloured as Ayers Rock, only lacking the majesty of its bulk. The Olgas are yet another fantastic landmark of the Centre, formed by the cataclysms of another age and are found 48 kilometres to the west of Ayers Rock. The tallest of this group of huge humps is 546-metre Mount Olga.

King's Canyon is a mighty cleft in the George Gill Range. Situated 325 kilometres from Alice Springs, the massive walls of the canyon tower over rock pools and lush vegetation. The sandstone walls rise up to 300 metres and are spotted with abstract rock patterns carved by wind and water. From the top of the canyon a spectacular view includes 'the Lost City' and the valley known as 'the Garden of Eden'.

Designed and produced by
John Currey, O'Neil Pty Ltd, Melbourne
First published 1979
© (photographs) Robin Smith
© (text) John Currey, O'Neil Pty Ltd
Typeset in Australia by Publishers' Aide, Melbourne
Printed in Hong Kong